NEAR & FAR

Poems by DAVE SMEDLEY

to Kirsten and Peter

with love
Annie
xy
Will xxx

Copyright Dave Smedley 2021

All rights reserved

The moral right of the author has been asserted

Dave Smedley studied chemistry. But what he loved most was cooking, fascinated by the formulation and mixing of ingredients.

He later transferred this interest to experimenting, formulating products such as special structural timber adhesives and high performance timber coatings to support his other passion, the preservation of historic structures. In 1976, having worked in global manufacturing organisations, Dave started his own company Rotafix, which he and a small loyal team built into a successful business.

Rotafix, unlike other manufacturers, made only water-based products which contained no organic solvents: unique for the time. Now, because of Dave's influence, these products are internationally known as highly successful timber protectors.

During all these years, Dave wrote poetry. His poems were put aside. Until now.

CONTENTS

NEAR 1
Nearness 2
Young expectations 3
Together 5
Thoughts on a dinner date 6
On growing young again 7
Once upon a dream 7
Second date 8
Please smile 8
Observation! 9
Please meet me in the park 9
Pleasant encounter 10
Just a word is enough 11
Courting refrain 12
The years in between 14
So easy to forget 16
Marriage 17
Meeting in peace 18
Freedom is not to be alone 18

FAR 19
Far and near 20
The years between 20

Separation 21
Separation 2 22
Walk in the woods 24
Death of a mountain man 25
Of iron men 26
Loneliness 27
Lady loneliness 28
Lady loneliness 2 29
Simon in the sky... 30

BETWEEN 31
Times forgotten, remembered 32
A new morning 33
Alone - together 34
Absence 35
Do not go away 36
Meeting at a distance 36
Lost 37
Falling in love 37
Pool 39
Time changed us 40
Close to good and bad 41
Chasing freedom 42
Semi-retirement 42
Friends for life.. 43

Being individual 43
Consider just the present 44
Comprehend just one feeling 45
Stage fright 46

TIME PASSING 47
Taking time 48
Hurry 49
Fill in time 49
Obsession wth time 50
Realising mortality 50
The leaf – recognition of mortality 51
Fleeting moment 52
Étoile et tricotet 53
Do not wait until tomorrow 54
Time waits for your answer 55
Time will not wait for me 55
Tide – disappearing treasure 56

THE NATURE POEMS 57
Banks of River Charente 58
To the sun 59
Sky 59
Spring so temporary 60
Early morning view 60

Butterfly 61
Nature's death 62
At night.. 63

THE LIVERPOOL POEMS 66
After all these years... 67
Memories of a quarryman 68
Liverp-hooligan poetry 69
Yesterday (once more!) 70

"Ah, but a man's reach should exceed his grasp, Or what's a heaven for?"

Robert Browning

NEAR

NEARNESS

Say it
with your eyes
I see them
Speak
Just a word
I listen to the silence
Say it with a touch
It will be part of me
Forever.

* * *

In the world of love between just two
There is no possible or impossible
Only the special logic of two lovers
Where numeracy and age are not to be found
The heart is so full that
Absence, distance and time
Only make you closer.

YOUNG EXPECTATIONS

We came together
all those years ago
I walked you home
You expected nothing

Annually we sat, we cuddled
We ate together
I offered you my future
You expected nothing

We worked and played
We married each other
I offered you my heart
You expected nothing

We lived together
We ate, we lay together
I gave you friendship's advice
You expected nothing

We lived our separate ways
We sometimes came together
I gave away your trust
You suspected nothing

We grow older and we
get wiser together
I insist on loving you
You are saying nothing

We could meet again tomorrow?
We would grow young together
I would offer what is left of me
And you will expect everything.

TOGETHER

Come with me to the bottom of the deep
Blue sea

Don't you see what is happening to the likes
Of you and me?

That is why you must follow

follow me

follow me

down, down

to the bottom of the deep blue sea.

* * *

You and me just floatin'
Floatin' in our world
Close to each other
Away from the others

With clouds just a floatin'
A glowin' bright

The heat of us and azure
blue
seems just right.

THOUGHTS ON A DINNER DATE

I don't know what to do, do, do
With this love that I have for you, you, you
I'm the captain of my ship
And they all call me 'skip'

Across the table for two
I wonder who I am?
What are you?

What am I doing here
without a smile or even a tear?

Where there is so little time remaining
in this game of entertaining

I love you so but it's not so clear
if you love me dear
or even a little – I would be sure
of happiness once more

So I drown my emotions
at the bottom of the oceans.

ON GROWING YOUNG AGAIN

Here she lies
My fresh-faced leaf
The maiden of
The trout pool eyes
Do not despise this glorious craze

You too are filled
With youthful fantasy
You have long been
And seem to be
Again
Light, nimble footed nineteen
Don't rush to seek
Old age twenty-one.

ONCE UPON A DREAM

Once upon a dream
there seemed to be
no end of sun
and you
and me

The water moves
incandescently
closer to
last night
and yesterday's tea.

SECOND DATE

When the world

turns around the world

We'll meet again

And know each other

just the same.

PLEASE SMILE

Don't run away
From the clown of this year

He makes you laugh
He makes you cry
At least he'll try

If you run
Leave your smile behind

Next year the circus
comes back to town.

OBSERVATION!

It must be the touch with love

When the feeling of warmth lasts
Almost until
the next
time

Whether it be three minutes or three months.

PLEASE MEET ME IN THE PARK

I seek not the trout pool stillness

nor the blue wastes of the soaring gull

or even the waving softness of the lily frond

Just the arm's length distance of your tiny hand.

PLEASANT ENCOUNTER

Come to me this way
like a butterfly upon the leaf
You touch me lightly
and fly away
Returning again and again

Then at last
the texture feels just right
and you stay
Maybe the wind
will blow you away
Please come back again
…. Maybe tomorrow

Anticipation thwarted
by cruel reality
The moment is upon us
What is the expectation
of one upon the other?
None
All is lost
in consummation.

JUST A WORD IS ENOUGH

It is also part of me
Tonight I give you just a word
I will give you a word to guide
you through the twilight

I will give you a word that is
A 'fish and chip supper' for a tired mind

I give you with a worn but gentle hand
A word
I place it on your furrowed brow
Don't move
Wait a while
Let it trickle down upon your cheek
Do not wipe it away
Let it rest upon your lips

Then sleep soundly
Let the word fall softly
quietly between your breasts
In the morning
you will wake
with all of your body
and then move
wrapped in 'hope'.

COURTING REFRAIN

It's not a song
but it's about you
I'm so frightened
that you are so
young again

I can't write a song
but it's about you
Walking in the rain
Holding your hand
keeps me warm
Touching your fingers
keeps me
thinking about you

Growing young again
will not make it the same
But it's about you
and this is
better
than not
growing at all
without you

Beside me, beside you
Beside me, love you
Time is a simple view
Panoramic clue
to the future
Would be a view
to the past

Search for the answer
Beside the solution
Presently
Beside me
Beside you.

THE YEARS IN BETWEEN

The years in between seem
Like a dream

We met at the terraced house ball
when I never knew you at all
The walking home
The walking back
was on fairy…
airy…
weary
footsteps

First step tremulous
Heart beating youth
Leaping passionate steps
seeking sleep

Passion unrational, irrational
waiting, making the hoping
Next time meeting
practised greeting

To lean forward and kiss
Or not?
Which would be
the plot?
Never wanting? Tempting? Hesitating?
Contemplating

Time was on our side
The world would provide
a ride
to the future.

SO EASY TO FORGET

So easy to remember
the first time I saw you

So easy to remember
the first time you spoke

So easy to remember
the first time I held your hand

So easy to remember
the last time we lived alone

A lifetime of yesterdays
has passed us by

I can't remember
the first time I made you cry

I can't remember
the first time I said goodbye

I can't remember
the thousand times I did not try

Now the second life starts
Let us forget these things together.

MARRIAGE

The start of the beginning
is the beginning of the end

So it is with lovers
but not with a friend

The start of the beginning will never end
when wife and lover
is your very best friend

Clock's hand on the wall
Calendars page by page
Crawling years.

* * *

The start of the beginning
is the beginning of the end for us

The time in between
is the start of both the end
and the Dream

We must make all
we can
you and I
To reach for the sun – together.

MEETING IN PEACE

We met at the terrace house ball
many, many years ago
Tomorrow follows yesterday
Follows the sun
When the world turns around the world
we'll meet
and know each other just the same

I seek not the silence of the airborne gull
Or stealth of the winter deer
nor even the depth of the deep pool trout
Only the peaceful times
of a quiet mind.

FREEDOM IS NOT TO BE ALONE

Freedom is easy
for one

The extravagance
Is the togetherness
of freedom
for two

More than twice the warmth
Is in the two of us

Alone there can never be anything
more than the whistle
of the cold, cold wind.

FAR

FAR AND NEAR

When you're near me girl
I don't need you here girl
When you're away dear
Far, far away dear
My heart says girl
You'll be back some day
Home to stay, stay, stay

You won't return to me.

THE YEARS BETWEEN

These were the happy years
These are the sad years
Feel the ecstasy, feel the pain
Again and again and again
The recollection of the sunshine
Washed down by the rain

Those are the memories
That are yours and yours
And mine and mine

Sadness remains.

SEPARATION

I feel the coldness of loneliness
on the edge of your smile
Mile follows mile
of desolate road

Communication is the end game
Remember, remember, forget
your name
Confusion helps me
retain part of you

More than twice the warmth
is in the two of us
Alone there can never be anything
more than the whistle
of the cold wind

I hope fervently
that in the silence
of your loneliness
you remember
the happiness
of times together.

SEPARATION 2

I feel the coldness of loneliness
on the edge of your smile
Mile after mile
of desolate road

Mornings of coffee
and toast
Back on the road
waiting for the weekend
the telephone call
tomorrow's post

In such a little time
I can make an untidy ending
And time after time
I try it all over again
and never unravel the thread

More than twice the warmth
is in the two of us
Alone there can never be anything
more than the whistle
of the cold wind

Communication is the end game
Remember, remember, forget your name

Freedom is easy for one
The extravagance is
the togetherness of
freedom for two

Hourglass biting
suddenly curled up
whirled up
tangled up
sleep

These images, these
explosive colours
provide a hidden
place for the
treasures of yesterday's thoughts.

WALK IN THE WOODS

The fir trees green and bright

I touched them here tonight

They swayed from left to right

They turned each way

Free

The movement wept with me

I feel no pain or shame

Just the thought that remains

of all the times that entertained

Please come back again

and love me

from another time.

DEATH OF A MOUNTAIN MAN

I want to die
here inside
he cried

Not out there
the lonely
only way

You give me
hope again
and then
you give me
pain

It's so sad
that I remain
outside your
domain

I'll come again
another day
and persuade you
to push the world
away

I have cried
I have died
The pain burns
Inside

I don't want you to die
I care for you
inside the me that cries.

OF IRON MEN

Amidst the senseless chatter
of our conversation
in the wrought
iron silence
of our missing communication

The noise closes down
on the silence of unsaid
emotion
Seared naked feelings
masking thoughts
considered inconsequential
Even mundane between
two bodies not so
well concealed

To us
so well versed
in self persecuting each other
inflicting pain

We cannot – I cannot – pass this furnace melting
molten metal way
In this or any other age.

LONELINESS

Another day
another road
I'm on my way again

I don't feel you
I don't feel the pain
but then
I'm on my way
On my way
Again.

* * *

Standing here outside your door
The smile is gone the pain returns
When you're here I don't need you
any more
when you're gone
I want you back again

Standing outside your door
The smile is gone the pain returns
I don't need you any more
But oh, I want you back again
The night is cold and dark
it's so lonely on my own.

LADY LONELINESS

I saw her standing
in the shade
next to the window
Loneliness wrapped in silk
against a curtain

She said "Hi there"
The sort of remark
not expected from
dark, silk clad
loneliness

I spoke from the other
side of the room
I reached out from
a mile away
Not thinking the touch was
Infinity
Not realising she was
Loneliness

"Not so close" she said
walking towards me
The silk moving closer to
her as she walked
Which way she went
I'm not sure.

LADY LONELINESS 2

I turned around too late
and caught just a glance
of the vanishing figure
as she filtered through
the door
leaving just a lilac scent
on the breeze she caused

I reached out and
caught the breeze
just a thread of the invisible silk
clutched to my chest

I was happy on my own
Lady Loneliness was gone
When the thread
becomes a dark smooth
silk dress
Then I know she
has returned again.

SIMON IN THE SKY

Where are you now?
My baby in the sky

In despair I press
salty eyes against
the clutched pillow

Your image will
not go away
Are you under the bed?
Don't reply

One day
When I have the courage
One day
When I find my way
to the sky

I'll find you
Whispering from
a cloud

I'll have found you —
then —
But I wish I had
you now
My baby in the sky.

BETWEEN

TIMES FORGOTTEN, REMEMBERED

It's only now that you are here
Remembering the times
that have been
forgotten by hurt
and memories avoided

I can't find the lines
that remind me of you

It's only now
when we remember the past
and acknowledge the mess
remembered by hurt
and thoughts admitted

It's only then
I can extend
the nearness of you.

A NEW MORNING

This morning is just like any other morning
Except
This morning you woke, reached
Across a thousand miles
And stroked my hair
For the first time in ten years

Yet this morning is like any other
Except
You said to me after the poem
What a lovely way to start the day
Yes, you did say this, I pinch myself
For the first time in fifteen years

This morning is just like any other morning
Maybe
When I stop dreaming the
day will be different.

ALONE - TOGETHER

It's for the very first time
The first time
we are alone
You and me
And now – what is there to do
alone
on our own

For the first time
on our own
We can think of
times gone by
and for the times to come

But alone is not the thing to be
We need to be together
You and me
For the last time
maybe forever
But whenever
it is to be
With you and me.

ABSENCE

All I hear is the flight of the bird
The silence of the night
walks, runs through
my mind – not a sound

All I ask of you
is that you should feel
gently towards me when
I feel close to you
I don't know when that
will be
But don't expect that
I should be there with you

My mind is strong
when you are absent
The argument appears when
you are there at my side.

DO NOT GO AWAY

Backwards in time
I can't find the lines
that remind me
of you

It's only now
when we know

That I think and vow
to extend the
nearness of you.

MEETING AT A DISTANCE

On the telephone
alone
talking at a distance
is like
The intimate touch of a familiar hand
You are here
but not quite near enough to touch
the presence of your secret thoughts.

LOST

What is my home?
When am I going there?

My home is in him and her and here

When am I going home?

Only when alone and I am there
do I think of home?

Is it a person, a place
or even a reason?

Perhaps my thinking
reasoning
is all because of the seasons?

FALLING IN LOVE

Coal is like a lover
or two
Perhaps two pieces
are me and you?

Coal is black
but you paint one piece white
It glows all shiny
day and night

Love starts with a light
It can start by accident
and that's exciting
or deliberately. Just
like coal with a match

Have you seen the fire
heaped with coal and dancing
with superhuman desire?
The fire
is great
Or is it in the grate?

The love that is fuelling lighting is unique
The flames are special
Don't let us speak
Let us feast on the heat
For when the flame subsides
despite what the world denies
the love and the flames have been
completed
Not even the shape of the
embers can be
repeated.

POOL

Swim with me
to the bottom
of the pool

Wheel like
eel like
wriggling
warmth

Touching you, holding me
reaching out
for softly
water wet
darkness

Down, down, down,
Come with me
Come with you

Only a fool
would stay
up there
where
it is forever
raining.

TIME CHANGED US

I knew you yesterday
It was so easy
when I could show you
what to do

Today you show me
the choice I have
Unlike you
I have no courage

I know you so well
I feel you so close
Our friendship association
and times together

I am glad you have grown
I am sad you have grown
I have given what I am
I have sold the soul of our friendship.

CLOSE TO GOOD AND BAD

The good feelings
are only just
a turn away

They hide
on the other
side of the
bad feelings

I look for
the courage
to turn the page

Without courage
I cheat
and see confusing
mirror writings.

CHASING FREEDOM

Yesterday

I walked across
next year's freedom

The feeling touched
me with fear

The loneliness
of today is left
in my soul

I will grow
old
with the thought
of freedom
yet to come.

SEMI-RETIREMENT

Last night I had this dream
I stopped travelling the old old scene
The time had come to stop
Like all the times before
But you don't believe me
Any more

I promise you
This time
It's true.

FRIENDS FOR LIFE

All I ask of you
is that you feel towards me
as gently as I do to you

I know it seems unreal
but that's the way I'll always feel

I know it's so sad
that I'm so bad
But one day we'll meet
and the world will be glad
we're not mad with
each other
any more…

BEING INDIVIDUAL

Tonight I saw you
Missed you
For the very first last time

I will miss you
See you again
For the last first time.

I'm so very glad that the memories
of yesterday
Don't fade and make you and I
Extinct

You do not need
A feeling hand
Or indeed a hand
To lead
Anytime.

CONSIDER JUST THE PRESENT

This start is the beginning
The beginning of the end
The joy of feeling tender
is the onset of feeling pain
Though it's not that sad

Yesterday is gone forever
We may have tomorrow to remember
today
But it doesn't matter anyway
The real memory starts here and
NOW.

COMPREHEND JUST ONE FEELING

Now we talk and walk
the long nights away
making every year
working by month
playing by day

Making it every year
working by month
playing by day
Now we talk
and walk
the nights away

Together we've made it
Made it on our own
Just understand one
feeling
of everyone we meet
Then one day
We'll know ourselves completely.

STAGE FRIGHT

Life has its many ways
of showing the world
valiant and dramatic plays
Enduring the floodlights of the
human stage

You may not know
on whose heart you have engraved
Unrewarded, take a bow

Dreams in vivid colour
accosted only by the more
rigorous joys of lasting
love
Wrought into the lasting
interference of those who will mother
next year's generation of lovers
going along with their sun.

TIME PASSING

TAKING TIME

It's past – well past
the time to consider
the remainder of the time

To consider
act and organise the
adventures
of a lifetime

Maybe the right time
to make the transition
of a lifetime

A lifetime of indecision
thinking and balancing
not taking the challenging
possibility of instant adventure.

HURRY

It may be tomorrow
and maybe it is yesterday

Which one?

The day is not to matter
It is the thought that is the reality
because time is not on our side.

FILL IN TIME

If you make it happen now
then there is a lifetime
between today and tomorrow

Just think how many lifetimes
you can live in the month
of June.

OBSESSION WTH TIME

An age and a half have gone by
in the time taken to stop
A tear, a smile
Perhaps

Turn away ....
Away from a world
obsessed
with time

Deadlines are
only obstructed by
confrontations
with speeding mortality
halted only and finally by
the unsuspected
speedcomer
of death.

REALISING MORTALITY

There was a time
not so long ago
when the word 'death'
brought pain
imagined pain
and real fear

Now the realisation
of mortality
and the real pain
of physical weakness
seems to discourage
Fear.

THE LEAF – RECOGNITION OF MORTALITY

I feel the new-born breath of Spring
This is such dynamism

In the interim, mortality
of my being
to lay open and checked
in sun and rain

To feel the perspiration running
from my veins
to my skin
and then
falling silently
on to the
floor beneath
Losing colour

All this being
is long past
protection.

FLEETING MOMENT

It can't last forever

not even for now

The longest moment has

passed us by and

down to earth you fall …

and some of me

So glad to be the

lovely

lonely

lucky ones

We know how sad we will be.

ÉTOILE ET TRICOTET

There are stars and there are stars
Some so distant
and yet for the intrepid
easy to be touched

My journey needs to be long
if I have even a remote chance
to grasp those untouchables

Please
I wish for a long journey
What good is it to arrive
without the miracle
of unknown
unexplained
experiences?
Better to disappear in anonymity

There is no easy route to a golden tapestry
Just the hard woven occasional
threads of gold amongst the
knit one purl one of life's
journey.

DO NOT WAIT UNTIL TOMORROW

Just around the corner
grows the greenest grass of my spring

Just around the corner
floats blue sky that ends my storm

Just around the corner
perches the nightingale that really can sing

Just around the corner
I will hear the cry of the first born

Just around the corner
my happiness follows an eternity of sorrows

Just around the corner
my easy living will come to stay

Just around the corner
you will say "I'm coming here tomorrow"
Just around the corner
all my life is happening today!

TIME WAITS FOR YOUR ANSWER

The less you do
the less time you have
to do a lot of
things you like

You have to create time
And that's a difficult skill
to develop

The lonely times
Don't remember me.

TIME WILL NOT WAIT FOR ME

Looking back to today's future
between today and yesterday
is a legend of memories
locked away and
forgotten.

Drowned by the persistent
actions of the present
pressured out of mind by
the constant emergence
of the race to
average human activity

The closeness of death
disaster
causes reflection.

TIDE – DISAPPEARING TREASURE

If only it will be
like this
when the 'real time'
arrives

There is a rainbow I see
But no, it is the
reflection in the window
It is on the other side

Travelling along with
the train across the
fields, hedgerows,
roads

Numerous pots of gold
gone -we have crossed
the estuary
The rainbow has drowned
in the sea.

THE NATURE POEMS

BANKS OF RIVER CHARENTE

She seems higher than the surrounding ground
The river
almost ready
to swallow the
banks on either side

Not through flood
or moon driven tide

The fullness of mud brown
belly flows undulating
from side to side

Perhaps some nude
but pregnant lady
Swaying this way and that
Glowing with pregnant pride
Smiling shivering complexion
Or is it perhaps a Cheshire cat
feline and lithe

Coaxing fishermen from the grassy
banks and
nearby cottages
to feel in the muddy waters
for small rewards of roach and
carp.

TO THE SUN

You are poised
serene and bright
This world's
eternal light
Which dries up nature's tears

The world is dark
before you appear
But you wrestle with darkness
only in fun
With a grinning face
and knowing fear
For always 'you' are the sun.

SKY

With clouds just a floatin'
a glowin' bright
The heat of azure blue
seems just right

Mist so slowly appearin'
Rain is a comin'
All is lost – quite soon
thunder a drummin.'

SPRING SO TEMPORARY

Verdant grass
motionless trees
Sun at last
gentle breeze

Birds whistle
flowers bloom
purple thistle
But autumn soon.

EARLY MORNING VIEW

Spring morning light

tells a chilly winter earth

all about our

rain storms and

sunny days

Producing a thousand

Perfect

Blooms.

BUTTERFLY

You come to me this way

The butterfly on limpid leaf

You touch me lightly

then fly away

returning again and again

and again

Then at last

the texture feels just right

You stay forever

and a day – NO

Maybe the wind

blows you away

Please come back again

Perhaps tomorrow.

NATURE'S DEATH

Here they are
Here they go
A million million
All in a row
Like the poet's
'Daffodils' in a
breeze they
suffer too
and lose
their lives

The leaves
they fall
to a better
call, they roll
Indeed, forever
Oh gentle soul
to a grave
They follow
in some
feral plain
or dismal hollow

Sleeping quiet
with lupus texture
the half dead
whistle with
undue shrillness
that breaks

the stillness
'til the heavens
open and
the last
sap of life
is drenched in
aqueous death.

AT NIGHT

The torrid heat of
Summer's day is fading fast
The artisan with grimy hands.
is homeward bound at last.
soon now the guardian sun
is plucked from the western heaven.
as Father Time marches on.
or it's nearly seven
Howling anger of monster traffic.
will soon now cease
and at the end of another day
the world is bathed in peace

High above in the black strewn murk.
plans are afoot
For the stars are ready for work
They throw down their bundle
of welcome light
And lo – born again is another
fleeting earthly night

Because ignorant man
thinks only of sleep
Hard working stars stay
guard over the fields of sheep

In the earthly sensuality of
moon glow
the lake is silently shimmering
together with lakeside trees
with Spring leaves so brimming
Evening dew descends in
flowing translucent crystals
as Mother Nature brings
forth the rigid purple thistles
But now! With great grasping arms
Black midnight calls
forth her sultry charms
She brings to bear the full
glory of her pure and loving heart
For only she knows the toll
and drudge of a new day's start

Because of this
the tall pine
and gem bespeckled terrain
look far more beautiful than any
of man's simple words can explain

The time has come for the pawns
of night to be readily blessed
as they come to the end of

another temporal rest
Creeping from the shadow
Of Mother Earth's flawless breast

The sun is inevitably
knocking at the bedroom door
Leave her alone; she is only doing her daily chore!
The moon fades out
in a desperate fight
For alas the triumphant
Sun is in her right.

THE LIVERPOOL POEMS

AFTER ALL THESE YEARS

I'd like to be me again
First ice cream
First Frankenstein dream
Not that first sickening cigarette
A sight of the present times
but the first beer 'n cider
or umpteen glasses of wine

I'd like to be me again
Running away from home
Reading comics on the throne
Escaping Auntie's head patting play
Dreaming of tea at the Adelphi
Going to Southport and ever receding tide
Eating candy floss and smelly donkey ride

I'd like to be me again
Front seat of the tram to Mere Lane
Collecting frogs and back home again
Making aquatic garden in the back yard
Practising conjuring and the disappearing cane.

MEMORIES OF A QUARRYMAN

I remember
screwed up eyes
in meek astonishment
Long corridor of cartoon murals
"You did that" says he (headmaster)
"Who, me, sir?" JL replies in mock astonishment

I remember
the visit to The Philharmonic –
Cultural of course!
John Ford's 'High Noon'
Usherette with shining torch arrives
Demanding of JL
Three times –
'What's your name? What School?"
In his usual unrelated style JL answers
"Yes missus I came on me bike"

I remember
underground at the locker room
The four handed card school
The other side of JL
'going blind'
after seeing the cards

I remember
the English class 1956
Harold Clubfoot (George Harrison)
"Sir, the 'new boy" JL says

is well up to standard for English Language GCE
You must enter him for the exam, Sir….he he"

Note: I was in the same class as John Lennon. George Harrison was a pupil at the Liverpool Institute Grammar School and his school had a day's holiday. Hence his presence at Quarry Bank.

LIVERP-HOOLIGAN POETRY

The quality of Mersey is not strained
with marmalade butties
and Tuesday's blind scouse
It imparts
to the inhabitants of the 'Pool'
that rasping nasal drawl
and the John Wayne gait

Sadly, Penny Lane
is no more
It has gone
metric
Or was it
metaphoric?

YESTERDAY (ONCE MORE!)

In moments of present time
forgetfulness
Memory provides the good times
once again
The last Liverpool tram rattles away to die
Hopscotch graffiti in the evening light
The timber blocks from the old road
We waited until dark and stole
the sacks of wooden coal
for the fire

The first romance in disused air raid shelters
The secret (very damp) meetings before each school day
She was pale with freckled face
wearing a gabardine mac
pinched in at belted waist

Under age secret drinks
and afterwards sickness
promoted by cigarettes

The excitement on gaining courage
to talk to those future Miss Worlds
in the forbidden school across the road

Hitch hiking youth
meeting the real people of the outside world

Growing up
Meeting you
Falling in love
Forgetting masculinity
Feeling you warm in bed
It all happened yesterday.

Printed in Great Britain
by Amazon